Some Days The Bird

Heather Bourbeau *and* Anne Casey

Beltway
EDITIONS

Some Days The Bird

Heather Bourbeau
and Anne Casey

Beltway
EDITIONS

Printed in the United States of America 10 9 8 7 6 5 4 3 2 1

Cover Art: Beth Moon
        bethmoon.com
        Dolby Chadwick Gallery
        info@dolbychadwickgallery.com
Cover Image: "Oak Seed #1"
Book Design: Jorge Ureta Sandoval
Author Photo: Heather Bourbeau
Author Photo of Anne Casey: David Clare, First Light Photography
ISBN: 978-1-957372-01-3

Beltway Editions (www.beltwayeditions.com)
4810 Mercury Drive
Rockville, MD, 20853
Indran Amirthanayagam: Publisher
Sara Cahill Marron: Publisher

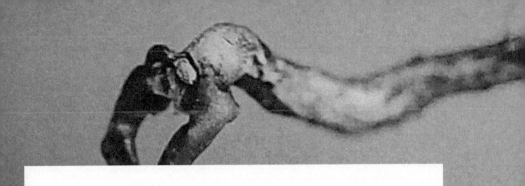

About the book:

Throughout 2021, as COVID and climate change battled for supremacy in the hearts and minds of the world, American poet Heather Bourbeau and Irish-Australian poet Anne Casey engaged in a poetry conversation back and forth across the globe, alternating each week, to create 52 poems over 52 weeks. With poems anchored in their gardens, they buoyed each other through lockdowns and exile from family, through devastating floods, fires, wild winds and superstorms. *Some Days The Bird*, a collection of internationally recognized and award-winning poems, is the result of their weekly communiqués from different hemispheres (and opposing seasons) in verse.

TABLE OF CONTENTS

The letting

by Heather Bourbeau

People have become numbers, corridors are morgues
and we are mocked by the tenacious need of green to grow—
jade blossoms repel rain, my lemon tree's grotesque fecundity,
my apple tree with patches of leaves, brown and golden, clinging
to branches that welcome the slow growth of lichen.

The soft rain a cleansing. Too trite a metaphor for this, this
broken dam of sorrow and relief pouring forth.
Some things cannot be forgiven. The cheapening of human life,
the persistence of oxalis, the failure to witness
when the lavender began to green.

I wake to a battle of squirrel and blue jay,
the leftover musk of skunk taunted by cat.
Above us, the conjunction is dissipating, but the wondrous
is not always this out of sight. This land, my fate
to be taught over and over again, I am not in control.

Coastal descant

by Anne Casey

Four hours north
of our new normal, a daily changing
tableau—already elsewhere from
the chatter and chant of ascending scales
in LA, London, Brazil; a sinkhole in Italy; a landslide in Java;
a plane fallen from the sky; wreckage
of the assault on democracy in DC—
we have hurtled out of city snarls
through eucalypt forests shooting
new green across the blackened scarline
of last summer's megafires, past vast shocks
of long-legged birds wading near wallowing gums,
their mottled trunks drowning in this year's floods,
to breathe again

clear air carrying a tincture of salt,
a trace of coastal rosemary,
count blessings falling like soft rain
on your remote lavender,
on my longed-for west-of-Ireland heathers
and here, on spiring cordylines, Norfolk Island pines
scraping a last skirmish of downy clouds,
their slender cones far below snagging
olive chains of Neptune's necklace
along the snaking tideline,

a sea eagle gliding high
over sands fringed in the wild fleshiness
of samphire, and higher over lobelia blooms

purple-tonguing rain-swollen air; where
blue triangles flit between the fresh dazzle
of golden Guinea flowers twisting
past ragged elephant ears
sagging in steamy strangler fig shade,
fishbone ferns filigreeing
the drifting sea breeze—
here where banksia trees turn into wind
off churning surf, their gnarled arms
spreadeagled into brine-laden sky,
contorting around rock, a symphony
of seed pods parrots a lorikeet's
brief speech, and a psalm of
cicadas echoes
wave-song.

The startling grace
of a rainbow's full cascade
into cobalt ocean
over a horizon thirteen thousand
miles from my home coast,
yet so uncannily alike;
a ghost crab dances *en pointe*
across our scarecrow shadows
before we swelter uphill
again through saltbush,
a cuckoo mocking
our blundering
passage

as three hundred metres below,
the small blot of a lone swimmer
sinks beneath the glistening surface—

a cormorant racing
its own shadow
over his
wake.

This is not an inauguration poem

by Heather Bourbeau

Yesterday, I woke to rain shadow winds, heat and fire and fear.
"We are too broken," my mind said. My body agreed, gave in.

On my apple tree, one leaf remained. It must have fought,
unaware its destiny—soft ground for ants and worms and me.

A cat mewled. A spider abandoned its web.
I miss the deer that walked into my yard.

If I had dug my hands into the ground, marveled
at potato bugs, felt the slick of slugs, mourned

the leavings of creatures who also call this home,
could that have soothed my reptile brain?

Today the crescent moon set early. The air is calm and crisp.
The leaf had fallen.

Inside, my peace lily prepares to bloom.

Our Prime Minister says the vaccine is not a silver bullet

by Anne Casey

Primordial monstera fronds list
in the blistering shade, a solitary
kookaburra silent between
the flagging liquidambar
branches scratching at my
lofty perch—even the cicadas'
earlier vigorous castanet stilled
to a relentless dull trill—a scorching
waft occasionally riffling his breast
feathers, downy white

as snow coating the slopes outside
my father's far-off window,
dusting his muddled head; icy sleet
piercing the winter
-pruned olearia where his cherished
blackbirds cluster on better days

and later here, the kookaburra will return
with his one true love and their
burgeoning brood to fill the swaying
evening branches
with their raucous laughter,

my heart rising to meet the updraughts,
torn between émigré anguish
and shimmering hope.

Richter's scale

by Heather Bourbeau

Rains have brought mushrooms, softened a thirsty ground,
mulched and heavy with greying leaves.
My neighbor's morning glory wraps round their trellis,

chokes trees that scratch my home, make roads for squirrels.
The earth shook last night, and I slept soundly soon after.
Should I worry—this messy line between accustomed
                                            and detached?

In my yard lie the remnants of my landlord's neglect—fallen
bits of roof, broken path lights, balls from children
grown and gone, a green toy soldier kneeling, rifle aimed.

Nasturtiums never planted sprout and spill, twisting
up my steps, covering what the oxalis cannot.
The sun has come too soon. I feel my throat prepare to parch.

Some days you're the seed, some days the bird

by Anne Casey

Through the gaps in the fence, I'm watching
a wattle bird bronco-riding a long, bobbing stem
—so absorbed in plucking plump rapture from the dark
crimson heart it's oblivious to the buck and weave,
purple floral spikes brushing its scarlet cheeks
like some portent from a forgotten fairytale,
essential ingredient in a witch's secret scheme.

Weeds thrive beyond the palings,
the grass thigh-high in places,
another sign of the times—
like the boarded-up shops
(one on our corner shuttered suddenly yesterday
after twenty-five years),
the half-empty city streets.

A shard of sun catches a dragon-fly's rise
over the fence. I saw some bush bees
there the other day
—the first in years since
the now-disappeared
council worker mowed
their cluster of wind-seeded crocus.

There are moments I'm consumed
by the jolt
of how our world has veered,
others bewitched by the hum
of wildness overcoming concrete.

Stow away

by Heather Bourbeau

Thick fog, light rain. Days like this, my hair betrays my roots.
Curls twist, gain momentum, desperate to drink every drop.

I rush to plant ground cover, to profit from the damp.
But the ants, they swarm in upturned earth, frantic for refuge.

One climbs into my sweater, waits for my tea to steep,
my legs to fold under thick blankets before attempting an escape.

I appreciate the effort, the careful plotting or headlong launch
that led to my unwitting transport,

but I have laid bay laurel and cinnamon at my threshold,
tightened all my caps, stowed honey on high shelves.

There is only so much outside I will let in.
The dirt under my nails. The echoes of fog in my hair.

The stillness of dying

by Anne Casey

hangs over every room in the house.
Outside, a thousand ponderous drops
glint from rain-bloated foliage,
the monstera deep green now,
fronds poised like over-sized ears.

My son's beloved
spiny leaf insect
has been losing her grip
for a week, unwilling to leave
his warm palm when
he gently lifts her back
into the lower branches,
where she will come
to no harm each time she falls—
until now, when we lay her
on a small bed of leaves
in the moist dirt,
the dark orbs of her eyes
following us, her pearly
peach cheeks,
apricot abdomen
and coral petal-wings
vividly belying
her decline.

Since early morning,
her sister has come to cling
an inch above her

downcast face,
front legs joined around
her bowed head, to linger
all day and through the night:
a hint there may be a whole world
of attachment beyond
our narrow understanding.

We will plant her under the Eucalypt
whose wide sweeping arms still
feed her small brood,
and leave
with the mystery
of her
and all
she left us.

Perseverance

by Heather Bourbeau

The Mars rover has landed. But for now, I am terrestrial.
My hands needy and dirty. Pull weeds. Expose beetles.
Unearth worms, touch their pink and writhing bodies.

In the campus clocktower, two peregrines prepare
to nest, their lives captured on webcam.
In my yard, two birds disappear into the lemon tree.

Do their wings carry the scent of citrus?
Does the echo of blossom rise to meet them
as they bend and burrow?

I learned the kiwi bird will sweep its bill,
back and forth, back and forth,
to find insects hidden among the leaves.

Turkey vultures will track the smell of decay.
Storm petrels follow the odor of krill.
A mother cow can smell her young six miles away.

I mark my mornings by inhaling strong tea,
my walks with bay leaves rubbed between palms,
my evenings by roasting sweet potatoes, baking bread.

One more day without the virus, I think and thank
my nose, aware this is not a foolproof test, that I,
like the worm, may find my body vulnerable,
my world upturned.

The federal government has extended the international border ban until June

by Anne Casey

A new coolness has crept
into the evenings, mornings
slower to warm, the long slow
hoot and lash—a whipbird missing
in small explosions of gold swarming
amongst branches still lush from last
month's late-summer rainstorms.

Underneath, dark glossy daggers
of the clivia defy already dwindling daylight
hours, thrusting their bright tangerine bells
at rakish angles as I shrink from news
pushing me unknown months further
from 'home' and my father waiting
patiently for his vaccine,

telling me how the birds are returning
to peck at the cat's discarded bowl
as he warms his ancient bones
in the freshly turned earth,
and I probe our narrowing
evening, the first curled fists
of fallen leaves grazing
the darkening lawn.

Equinox

by Heather Bourbeau

I prune Japanese quince, grieve the past we never had,
place clippings in vase, stare at impossibly coral leaves, wonder
how I never before noticed these blossoms,
these harbinger kin of my plums.
The days grow longer, more languid.
I cross streets, my hands recoil.

It has been one year. The presidential screeds are gone.
Along with a half million of my countrymen.
More than World War II, we are reminded when we can bear
to hear the burden. In March 1945, the US firebombed Tokyo.
Killed 100,000 Japanese. Left one million homeless.
No one served time for war crimes then either.

My arm is sore from the vaccine. My mind a fog.
But the muscles of my heart expand. Soon I will hug others
like me. The vaccinated. The survivors. The grateful.
Today is the equinox. I hike Mt. Tamalpais, follow the path
of Snyder and Ginsberg, bow forehead to meet red wood.
Hear the rain-full creek. Smell the ocean's brack.

The Minister for Bushfire Recovery is reassigned to Floods

by Anne Casey

To our north, a wedding couple watch with
countless millions as their connubial
home drifts slowly down the swollen river,
as fifteen thousand neighbours are evacuated
from their coastal community, where we basked
in beachside sunshine only weeks ago.
To our west, the mountain road I commuted daily
for seven years has slipped into the gully,
closed for the foreseeable future, friends
on either side of the great divide
marooned between mudslides.

Southwest, the city's main dam is spilling
over a year's water supply each day.
Our waterlogged lawn is awash
with motley foliage debris, fat silver
globules shimmering from every
moisture-glutted leaf surface,
fairy-lighting the fringe of the veranda

where a week ago I watched our dog
stand stock-still for a long while,
gazing out into the distant
skyline as if in praise
of the balmy evening's
languorous descent,
a swoop of sulphur
-crested cockatoo

alighting like
candles in
the waiting gum
(echoed in monstera
blooms flaring out of gloom),
first heralds of an electric
storm brewing in the pinkening
dusk—sub-rosa

presage that this country has more tricks
up its sleeve than the slickest
sideshow illusionist.
Tomorrow, they say,
this pummelling rain will
magically stop and sun
will once again
split rock.

Into the loam

by Heather Bourbeau

I dig on borrowed land, unearth seeds and rusted
nails, blanched stems of doomed plants.
Newscast says *prepare for historic drought*, and
I wonder what that means anymore.

I dig and search for veins of covered creeks.
The Strawberry. The Codornices.
Tenacious steelhead trout still
spawn in the echoes of these waters.

I dig further and sift through acorn dust and bone.
Thirsty. For guidance, for redemption, for answers
too late for seeking. Should I water
the young primrose? Purple and pink.

And if I dig deeper down, I may crack upon
the bones of camels, the memories of mastodons.
Musk ox and ground sloths. Recall that, before eruptions,
this was savannah, wide and wet and flat.

I steel myself for the coming language—
burnt and *blistered, whipped* and *ravaged* cocked and ready.
Grateful green leaves emerge from my near-bare tree,
hummingbirds still feast on my sage.

Our Prime Minister stands by

by Anne Casey

his man: his Attorney General
accused of rape, as one hundred thousand
women march against gendered violence.

> Backing out of the garage,
> I am sometimes distracted

> by a piercing white glare,
> as yesterday—

the rare eruption
from the muted, glossy duck
-green leaves of a *Magnolia Grandiflora,*
the immaculate, incandescence of a solitary
flower coronet spilling light out of murk—

> a singular radiance often
> best observed from above

> > (my neighbour occasionally admiring
> > one from the height of her balcony).

I have come to search the shadowy underbelly
of the shrubbery, amongst the rusty understory
for that sudden delicate swell—to be stopped mid-flight,
breathe in its silky luminescence, delicate citrus notes
perfectly poised over the headiness of sodden mulch.

> Overnight, great fistfuls of rain pounded down,
> leaving a small, bruised heap on the ground:

dark branches fill my rear-view mirror as our
Prime Minister says
it was a triumph our women's marches
weren't met with bullets.

Tomorrow, I may call on my neighbour,
suggest a cuppa on her upper balcony
where we might sit looking down across
the *Magnolia Grandiflora*, gazing
out of our sixth and eighth
decades, over this country

long at war with
its women.

Pause

by Heather Bourbeau

Each year they come, the grasses.
They force cracks through my path.
Perhaps I should admire
their need to survive and grow,
then yellow and die.
Instead, each year, I rip them out,
make space for flowers.

Next week will mark my menopause.
One year since my last sloughing.
I see the drain of estrogen
in my eyes, my skin, in the small belly
fat above my pubic bone.
And in the wisdom that comes
when one is not only driven to fuck.

This spring, I will keep one patch
of grasses and wood sorrel
floating between my brick
as a reminder to delight
in things we have been taught
are not worth savoring,
hold no value.

Evensong

by Anne Casey

Half a lifetime ago,
I sat goggle-eyed through
a *wayang* shadow-puppet show
      in Surakarta—enraptured
      by the spectacle, only part
      -picking up its threads.

Slanting pink-gold
these past evenings
through the autumn-thinning mantle
      of our backyard trees, edging
      between moth-eaten monstera fronds,
      fading cornets of the clivia, curling lace of tree ferns,

across distant eucalypts
waltzing to a stiffening breeze,
dusk-lit silhouettes are full of stories:
      this nightly theatre backlighting the invisible
      threads that have pulled us through
      our days—

            new-born squalls,
          tricycle spills, first readers,
       high school exams, gratitudes alongside
     acceptances of losses, almost twenty anniversaries—

and I am frozen looking out;
twin moon-bright saucer-eyes:
a ring-tail piggy-backing her joey
      past our window pauses, a cacophony

of kookaburras is silenced in the boughs,
and I wonder:

        Was this the beginning
      of worship millennia ago—where
    we found the faith to carry us through
the shadow-world to whatever might lie ahead?

All the while,
the clatter and rush
of people going home
    or heading out, fewer
    overhead than before:
    a reminder we can take nothing

for granted
as the light drops,
half the planet rotating away
    from what sustains us,
    the dog's ears stiffening
    for a single engine sound.

Perigee

by Heather Bourbeau

I wake to a congregation I cannot see.
Standing on my threshold, I am stilled, aware
of calls, once cacophonous now distinct—

the Bewick's wren trills, the mourning dove coos,
the Steller's jay claiming his territory, calling his mate.
Apple blossoms burst and fall. Pink and white.

Tonight, we welcome the Pink Moon,
the Egg Moon, the Grass Moon, the moon
that marks the return of hope and renewal.

The perigee a tease. The Farmer's Almanac says
now is the time to kill weeds, cut timber,
thin, prune, plant.

The rains have come just in time to try
and wash us clean, but the moon does not care
about our winters and our wretchedness.

We think one conviction will dig our ugly out,
thin the rotten ranks. But one is not enough
to quell roots wily, well-fed and still so hungry.

Autumn shades

For Joe

by Anne Casey

A chill south easterly is buffeting the last
of the rhododendrons, lodging their
gaudy protest against autumn's steady progress,

stirring memories of other rhododendrons far away
among the winding lanes of Mount Callan,
boughs meeting overhead, to dissect
the sky into glinting shards,
a glitter of lake reflecting here and there
between the lush profusion of blooms
—violet, cerise, lilac, cloud-white—walking
side-by-side with my father,
the shadow of grief still circling

his hollowed eyes, deflated cheeks,
his tentative feet barely touching earth
along this grass-grown road he had strolled
so many summers arm-in-arm with my mother,
clutching you then in his great powerless hands,
your fine platinum strands drifting on lake-breath
to tickle his bristly cheek, and—as if you knew—you threw
your head back, electric-blue eyes crackling
a silent current between you, your small fists hinging,
lit face wide-open to take in all those wondrous
new colours, a lone red wellie-boot stranded
somewhere on the trail behind.

I never cut fresh flowers from our garden
although, almost year-round, I could have my pick—

camellias, clivia, hibiscus, gardenias, lily-white monstera
cones, the delicate pink bells of the *Elaeocarpus Prima Donna*
ragdoll-dancing on the breeze, jacaranda lilac-carpeting
                                        the path,
Magnolia Grandiflora and frangipani perfuming the air—
their names as lovely as their sudden unfurlings.
I like to watch them linger, fade on branch
or stem, alongside the newly budding.

Maybe after school I will show you
our late-bursting rhododendrons,
tell you how once, before you can remember,
you salved your grandfather, taught him
how to carry his living
together with
his dead.

Twine

by Heather Bourbeau

Fog rolls in, burns off.
Signals early heat in the Central Valley.
The plums are budding. My mouth already craving
tart sweet, the fretting over so many.

There is one long branch on my apple tree.
I want to rest my weight against it, feel its support,
touch the lichen and bark and scars from pruning.
Breathe in. Apologize. My temple to its.

At 17, my friend Peter and I would wander at dusk.
In Capitol Park, we climbed oaks and madrones.
Smelled rose and sage, sap and summer heat.
Shared dreams and visions, coiled these round the barks.
And waited. For our firm thighs to run.

By afternoon's slanting

by Anne Casey

the cracks are showing—
a sapium leaf caught in full,
late-autumn sun displays
its x-ray plate of capillaries,

    a leaf-curling spider's lair
    alight, its delicate thread
    -work revealed with all its
    weather-worn flaws.

A woman of a certain age
shuns direct sun.
The amber flame
of a cicada skin,

    lit from within,
    still clings
    in the fraying
    fringes of the casuarina:

while yarning together,
a D'harawal woman taught me
not to call it by its other name—
a blight on all women.

    Some days I long to sink
    my wind-parched hands
    wrist-deep into moist black loam,
    daydream of digging heedlessly

through razor-sharp shale
to submerge in murky
subterranean lakes,
abandoning time, to tumble

       through jagged crevasses
       into that raging core and
       emerge reforged amongst
       your apple-tree's tangled roots.

The rim of my hat snags
a wriggling larva swinging
from invisible silk:
returning me

       to the creak of
       these softening bones
       and everywhere this molten
       golden light.

Watching the grass grow

by Heather Bourbeau

The hunched cat mewls at phantom squirrels,
cries for birds that have not come today. Then leaves.

For a moment, I mistake this for quiet.
I scratch myself on a thorn I do not see

for all the lemons mixed with roses.
Then I notice the fig now bent in supplication,

the apple tree suddenly bare of blossoms.
I strain to see new starts rise through earth,

witness the peel of bark, hear leaves unfold
on branches. For a moment, I am like an absent father,

aware what little part I play in the miracle
I almost ignored.

It is the first of winter

by Anne Casey

and all the liquidambars
have cast off their crowns,
golden stars drifting down
for weeks to shroud the listless
grass, clumps of crumpled rust
piling up on every outdoor surface,
my sons' half-hearted forays to rake,
heap, cart engulfed by autumn's implacable
advance, now given way to winter,

windblown piles of flesh, yellow,
brown, red laying waste to the shrivelling
lawn where I am standing now as I wonder
how many have fallen, what three and a half
million looks like: more than this I know.

A few days ago I saw the super blood wolf
moon looming out of a cloudless black night,
resisted the urge to howl. The illusion of its
giant peach face thrusting at us, retreating as
the chill seeped in, my younger son returning
outside over and over as if for the first time
realising some things don't last, not everything
is on tap, that we are all living on borrowed land,
borrowed time.

Sometimes I wonder if this
is what drowning in space
sounds like or screaming
in deep water. If you watch

a duck gliding across
the flawless surface of a lake
for long enough, you can see
its webbed feet pummelling
the glass underside.

I turn back to the warmth
of the kitchen, the dog hot
on my heels, a withered leaf
swinging from his whiskered grin.
Maybe if we stick together,
we might just shake
this thing off.

Revelations

by Heather Bourbeau

The crows are screaming.
Two tricksters taunt.
I spend my days peeling my protections.

Masked and hatted, I am no one and everyone.
And so, crow dives, hits my head.
I look up, lower my mask as if to say,

"I am not the one who wronged you,"
but he knows what I do not want to admit—
every day I am complicit.

Yesterday, in the full sun, a coyote,
skin and bones, youth and madness,
crossed the highway, confident, hungry.

We were naïve, even when we weren't.

And here I am again,
ready to make a spectacle of my guilt,
rather than seek our salvation.

Today I sit among the rose and ficus,
sage and fig, buds that will become apples,
weighted limbs of the plum ready to drop.

Like a young child,
I point and say, "Green,"
as if that were enough,

as if it were not magic, this alchemy
of turning one gas into another,
my breath into theirs.

A rogue polar outbreak

In loving memory of Bridget Lonergan
by Anne Casey

has breached our locked borders, dumping snow
in the Sunshine State, record lows all over, icy floods
receding to reveal a sprawling veil of spiderwebs
across Gippsland, quicksilver as the chill
stripping our garden of colour: the last lingering pink
camellias now browned and crisped on their stems;
the emaciated lawn has given up the ghost;
skeletal phalanges scratch at an ashen sky,
a single scrunched star still dangling stiffly
from the liquidambar's bereft grip

as we cluster for warmth indoors,
bunches of her favourite colours
peering over our shoulders:
purple, lilac, lavender, fuchsia
perky as summer beaming from screens
ablaze in phosphorescent greens back 'home'
where three generations gather to mark her passing.

Mother of six, first known world to my own love,
she who had known how to give when you have nothing.
Magnanimous grandmother to ten, once
award-winning gardener, her legacy now thriving
on three continents, in opposing seasons,

by the grace of her strong hands,
no matter the prevailing conditions.

Kin

by Heather Bourbeau

Before the solstice, I dreamt of a tsunami,
the shoreline pulled back, brazen,
exposing her shells and seaweeds, and no one
stopped the party to run to higher ground.

Unlike the spiders who climbed and wove blankets
of high web across Victoria after the floods.
Here, I save my shower water, wipe webs from my rafters,
my bicycle, my car's rearview mirror.

When we are infants, Lacan said, we believe
everyone is an extension of ourselves.
We do not understand why we cannot meet
our unspoken needs.

On Father's Day, I drove and shopped and cleaned.
And as I scrubbed debris of my father's body
from his shower, his toilet, we listened to the radio.
My yellow gloves paused, my dad's breath periodically

fluttering in a half-snore as I heard
an Afghan refugee speak of her father's torture,
the extraordinary measures he took to ensure
her safety and passage to this country.

I wiped tears and for a moment, watched
my own sleeping father.
I think of my Australian friend's forced separation
                              from her Irish dad,
her husband's losses of both parents during this pandemic.

These are the small silver threads tethering us—
empathy and gratitude.
A mother deer and her two fawns come
to eat my apples that drop to the dry, dry earth.

Storming our perimeter

by Anne Casey

Delta has sequestered half
our country as I gaze out
at a most un Sydney dawning

      after reading of Jakarta's great loss:
      so many little ones ghosted
      away.

This palest silver-blue-grey:
an Emily Dickinson kind-of-sky—is casting an eerie edge

      to everything as I kiss my sleeping
      children; beyond the branches'
      abandoned grasp,

the district is emerging
from an overhanging
fog, that had swathed us

      in its seductive
      phosphorescent trousseau;
      suffused now in a sort of hyperrealism,

the unearthly stillness, the city's
unaccustomed silence
is echoing through—

      after weeks of drizzling rain,
      the garden is full
      of broken things.

Threshold

by Heather Bourbeau

Lately, I anticipate a deer.
I walk through the dried grasses crushed,
the volunteer mint green, the apples strewn, whole
                                    and half-eaten.

I expect the doe, now grown, patient, waiting
to be let in, my right arm to brush against
her short, silken fur as I press past to open the door.

For a breath, I am sad to enter my house without her.
The flies and bees and spiders, though,
they always find a way inside.

Once a bird crashed against my window,
and my heart stopped from the shock
before we both shook it off.

Sydney stay-at-home order tightened

by Anne Casey

Our world has shrunk
to the brink of the sleeping
garden where monstera fronds
slump like fallen combatants,
a fine white mist disappearing
the universe
beyond our fence—
only one person is allowed
to leave the house once per day
for necessities.

People have started dying again—
at 11 each day the ticker-tape races
to parrot the premier's tallies.
Another woman my age died
suddenly yesterday after AZ
as the chief medical officer tells us
to take our second shots:
as if we aren't caught
between two devils
we don't know,

the clivias have thrown out
one or two
anaemic blooms
that shrivel quickly in the
winter chill; we had a good run,
but we squandered our lead.
(Like climate change, we failed

to read the signs.)
It's an ill wind, but I don't miss
the traffic noise.

> *What if this is it*
> *but we don't see it yet?*

Against the barren lattice of the trees,
the sky presses its pale face too near
like a great wraithed mirror
checking us for breath.

> *If a poem falls in a forest*
> *and no-one is around,*
> *does it still make a sound?*

Maybe that would be the ultimate poem.

Lughnasadh

by Heather Bourbeau

When I was a young woman, I was asked—
Imagine yourself an animal.
Others chose hunters
nocturnal, avian, feline, hungry.
I knew my ears were large, my heart fast,
my hooves ready to leap at every sound,
each trauma training me toward the cervine,
the prey.

I rip the wild grasses,
trim sage and lavender,
mourn the globe amaranth
that did not survive the drought.
My ancestors climbed hills,
buried flowers or corn,
slaughtered a bull
to mark summer's end,

dark nights on their way.
The harvest is starting.
I seek storage for apples—
sauce, butter, breads, dried.
Lemons rot on the ground.
Outside, we eat and dance,
friends and strangers,
almost celebratory,

while delta floats in time.
So many years unlearning
alert, long hikes alone,

studying tracks and scat,
until I could breathe in,
full and pleased. I have always
been more comfortable among
bear and lion than man.

(*Lughnasadh* is an ancient Celtic feast to mark the start
of the harvest season.)

Conversations with my father

by Anne Casey

The dying sun is sketching
   the neighbour's trees
      in charcoal on our bedroom wall

      in a last surge of pale amber
   as I follow my father between
pots of gold, purple, fuchsia

and flaming orange,
   the small brown wren hopping
    ahead, his ancient
      ginger cat grumbling
          over his missing breakfast,

    sunlight flaring between
    fistfuls of vigorous foliage
    as he shows me his bounty of strawberries—
Never mind the earwigs
he is saying as he plucks a pocketful *for Catriona*
   up the road: the children love them
    with a sprinkle of sugar—
   and *They keep the slugs at bay, aphids too,*

    the earwigs I realise as he ambles
   to the tangle of blackcurrant bush,
  draws back the emerald curtain
to reveal clusters of darkening orbs—
the blackbirds are busy looting
  further in, he tells me:
   Let them have their fill,

drawing me past the swell
    of wild roses as I lean in to inhale
      the scent of nothing,
     gasp obligingly at the grace
   -ful sweep of his ivory lilies:
I'll bring some to your mother
when I go to weed the grave,

as I dutifully inspect the ripening apricots,
   grapes thronging the shrivelling vines,
    chirp brightly as I find myself

        drifting

   from room to room in our dark house
  with him
beaming from my palm.

Artificial fire (Feu d'artifice)

by Heather Bourbeau

Every night, illicit fireworks explode.
Every night I fear guns and fire,
shake metaphorical fist at fools
who need this spectacle, who would dare
the gods to bring Hades to these hills,
before putting in my earplugs,
playing the chirp of crickets,
the lull of waves.

I have become what I used to pity—
Bradbury's Mildred Montag,
needing her ocean of sound to calm
her *unsleeping mind.*

In the morning, I drink thick, sweet tea,
listen to Umm Kulthum, reach for my glasses.
The mother deer in my (her) garden
arches her back, stops, (is her breath held,
as mine is?), then rotates her ears
in opposite directions, before we both find
blue jays alighting on dried nasturtiums
(*kindling*, I think and then, *do not jinx it*).

We watch each other watching.

Fawn and mother nibble the green
of new weeds, the apples untouched
by squirrels. If they would ask, I would say
Eat it all. She licks her child's ear,
bends, pick nits with her teeth on the neck,

the rump, then back to the ear.
I want to sleep to these sounds—
the soft lapping of tongue on fur,
the tiny click of tooth on louse.

Just past midwinter

by Anne Casey

They have started
to fall—
   the small
      brown spheres

            with their skins of spikes
            and hearts of seeds—
            the liquidambars'
      treats

      that will summon
rainbow lorikeets
   in their droves
      to cluster, gorge, *screech.*

         Nearby I have seen
         lotus trees fill the blue
      sky with their prayers
   of pink and white,

our rhododendrons paying
      purple homage
            to the return
               of sun,

               three brown streaks
                        spearing through

         the bud
         and chitter
      erupting all around
   after so much grey.

There   is
a screech—a   small
spiky   wooden ball
clutching   seeds—that
might frighten   my children,
alarm the dog,   scatter the
lorikeets   who have   just
now   swooped   in
to gorge   on our
greening lawn

if I fail
to contain it
here, at the centre
of my being.

The golden hour

by Heather Bourbeau

The smaller bee prefers my aging lavender,
hops between blooms, nuzzles each calyx.

The other bee, invasive and immense, swirls
across my path, drunk on a sea of purple sage.

Now I am partial. This *apis* has found
my tender bit, the corner of my garden

I will defend beyond reason,
the flowers I still run my fingers through

most mornings to drink their scent,
the hedge twisted and greying

that I still trim each winter in hopes of
coaxing one more fragrant return.

My apples are dropping, culling the runts,
so those that remain will sweeten and grow.

They crash around me, these petulant children,
demanding my attention, but me,

I keep witness to tonight's
last slurp of nectar.

New South Wales on a knife-edge amidst soaring numbers

by Anne Casey

A squall of miners
is bombarding the interloping
lorikeets, a honeyeater
higher up, quietly raiding
seed-pods swinging
in premature spring sunshine
between eruptions of tender
apple-green leaf-buds.

Over the top of our fence,
the neighbour's bougainvillea
is waving bright pink
salutations to the season's
over-hasty arrival,
her elephant ears straining
at my closed window.

Even the pots edging
the verandah have
surged into urgent
growth, succulents
over-running rims to
probe the weathered pavers,
the orchid (long missing-in-action,
assumed-dead) suddenly bursting
with buds, a flurry of ivory petals discreetly
unfolding under the busyness of pillaging birds.

But I am not ready to throw off
my winter threads,
fly free from my
delta-guarded parapet—
there are signs these days
are still too much like
a dip in my far-distant
native Atlantic: all warm patches
and cold drifts.

When fire became a season

by Heather Bourbeau

Ash rains softly, coating sleeping cars.
In another lifetime, we might have imagined
dandelion dust blown by giants
making wishes.

Sierra child, I grew chasing snow, laughing
as small flakes fell onto my willing tongue.
Now, under eucalyptus, I stifle instinct
to tilt head, capture fog dew. Thirsty.

I miss the touch of romantic partners.
Instead, I pet stripping blue gums, madrone,
remember the scent of wet high desert pine, juniper.
Mourn the losses.

Last night, I dug out the dead starts and stalks,
laid fresh soil, tucked in white sage, marigolds.
The sign at the nursery said, "Plant now
for Day of the Dead."

To see an owl in the day, wisdom must come

by Anne Casey

Over the heads of baby
pink camellia flowers,
I heard an owl hooting
over and over
in broad daylight:
wondered what it meant,

the morning after full of groans—
long, slow, constant, gut-wrenching—
a giant steel claw scraping raw
rock since dawn across the gully
where just weeks ago
a cluster of gumtrees
gave praise to
swarming
rainclouds,

the hollowed socket
of a rhino skull
eyeing me
from the bathroom floor,
an emaciated vulture
circling above—shivering
shower-water, I saw
my footprints had
erased them both—

even the electrical sockets
are ghosting
existential
screams,
headlines screeching,
the cloud full
of warning

beyond our
watchful trees
as sundown
shrinks
into a thin red line
before darkness
swallows it whole:

our kind, always good
at reading omens
in shadows—
so much better
at ignoring them
now.

Congregation

by Heather Bourbeau

The abandoned raised wooden boxes are gone,
given to a neighbor who has chosen a religious life.
I am struck by his youth, this man who has chosen
communion over copulation.

I wipe my feet, brush my jeans, my legs, my hair—
aware I have disturbed the earwigs under the piles.
At night, together, they will dive into the earth,
eat the entropy of decaying leaves.

Before I sleep, the fawn dives into the agapanthus,
its hooves and teeth tearing at the tall stems.
Not only for crickets and rats, this dark.
All this earth moves underneath me.

In the morning, the crisping air is not yet cool enough
to lull the hummingbirds into delicious torpor.
And so, outside before the latening dawn,
we inhale the fog together.

I learn that hummingbirds do not form flocks
even when migrating. I stare at the blue-throated and Anna's,
wonder if their solitude is to spare us
the pain of too much beauty gathered at once.

Days of wild weather

by Anne Casey

had battered our windows,
furious gusts stripping plump
purple blossoms from the burgeoning
wisteria to scatter them across the rippling
lawn; newly burst leaves flaying wildly
on the towering trees as they arched
into flailing winds and lashing rain—

I fell asleep to the mighty roar,
the crack and smash of branches
battering our ink-eyed skylight,
dreamt of phosphorescent starfish
racing through storm-ravaged seas,
stirred to the dog pining at my feet,

woke to the surprise
return of spring,
heart filling with the chitter
and chirp, swoop and shimmer,
wattles overnight had exploded
their bright saffron puffs,
the liquidambars' early leaves
now turning their tender starfish bellies
to the warming sun,

all the earth,
it seemed,
singing its song
of survival in whatever
narrow corridors
we allow.

Return

by Heather Bourbeau

A week ago, a young father was taken by the water.
We wait for the return of his body.
The Potawatomi say the reservoir

is a noun only if water is dead.
Otherwise, it *is being the reservoir.*
In English, I understand *Your mother is grief.*

This is not the order of things.
I pass neighbors and strangers and think,
May your children outlive you.

The acorns are browning,
beginning to fall.
To eat the flesh, you must first leach

out the tannins.
Raw is death.
Water is life.

We will gather in high desert
where the hideous irony will not be lost
among us, the parched.

At sea level,
in a moment of grace,
soft rains have arrived.

I gather drops,
run thin wet fingers through greying wet hair,
gasp at the shock of a rainbow.

On Sunday

by Anne Casey

we left wintertime behind,
woke to a lost hour,
reset the clocks
to hurry on
the approach of summer—

the reincarnated
orchid has put out
great festoons like clouds
of ivory butterflies,
the first monarch of the
season perched on the edge
of one blanched lip flexing
its stained glass wings:
ember-bright, black-rimmed
as the midnight shots
of lava consuming
Canarian villages.

I lost a whole day once
adrift with a thousand others
somewhere between Jakarta
and Medan, several weeks
over thirty years
on the wing between
Sydney and west Clare,
months on end
between
head
and heart.

One hundred days
into lockdown,
time is measured
in wingbeats,
aeons.

I am here and not here:
my missing time measured
in lost dollars living
on unlent land
whose true custodians
understand we coexist
in all time, this earth
converging through us:

I live long ago and now
far away and here, which are
the same, simultaneous
in me; my people
walk with me—all
of my lost and found here
together

looking out
at these trees,
feet suspended
in pulsing layers of
decaying moments,
a million green wings
flapping in the buzzing
air, their outstretched
limbs holding up
this blazing
universe.

Settling

by Heather Bourbeau

This is how we prepare for the death of winter
with fire warnings and pumpkin spice.

The squirrels are fattening.
Apple debris and green acorns.

I hear the winds before I see their wake
and wonder if calm will ever not be

just "before the storm."
Crackling leaves and nasturtium buds.

I hear the titmouse and the towhee.
Two hummingbirds dive and cross.

A whirr of red and green
before I notice the long-neglected roses

that will need to be pulled one day.
But not quite yet.

A time to reap

by Anne Casey

La Niña has sent three
hulking black brush turkeys
to huddle on the sturdy lowest limb
of our billowing backyard tree—
brutal gusts ripping fiercely
through lush foliage;
a honeyeater thrown from cover
flips vertical, plummets
beyond the whipping
bougainvillea.

All day, the dog frets,
tail trailing kitchen tiles,
constantly under my feet,
my windpipe constricting over
my part in the unfolding
spectacle, blood-tied
to this relentless
race.

Two cranes break
the skyline over the heads
of our besieged
neighbourhood trees:
red lights blink
constant warning
from their hunched necks
all across the district;

between wind swells,
the sound of a dog
barking alarm
somewhere amongst
thriving native growth
echoes up from the gully
now slated
to be cleared.

Meditations on a storm

by Heather Bourbeau

A river is falling from the sky.
Lazarus creeks return in rushes.
Safe inside, I watch the green against grey
bend and drip, drip and bend.

I want to say I think of rising reservoirs,
animals returning to higher ground,
next year's fruits and grains,
the burden of fear lightened a little.

But I prepare for ants,
desperate. Their nests flooded,
my house dry.
I lay bay leaf, defend my pantry.

I want to say I can trace this water
from Sierra headwaters surging
to delta through dams and aqueducts,
from plants to faucet;

that I thank those who carved and cored,
dreamed and dammed and drained,
those who purify and protect so that I
may flush my waste, drink from tap;

or that I recognize those displaced and dead,
learn the fields and fauna, lush and lost
never to come back so that I may live
beyond this land's means.

But today I make tea and dream of
longer showers, spectacular hikes.
Leaves and branches, oil and feathers
gather in gutters, float to Bay.

My friend says, *I tried to start a hemlock poem*
and I recall a time before I understood thirst,
when new friends gathered flowers,
offered to make a tea, before the wisest among us

identified the poison.
This rain will revive fields of French broom, fennel,
and hemlock. White lace, delicate and beautiful
as it chokes the yampah and blackberry.

Season of Samhain

by Anne Casey

Shadows are racing,
racing across the distended bodies
of the monstera, a merciless ruckus
in the highest branches of the quivering gums
as I search this second morning of November
for messages from my dead

in the teeth of a bitter
breeze, the seething
hiss and whisper passing under
a hundred bluish lips, amongst
the jacarandas' first cautious offerings
to this immortal season.

Last night I might
have followed after my late mother
in quiet vigil, lighting
rows of tealights to lick the edges
of cut glass passed
down from her own late mother,
shades lifted,
a window cracked,
cups poured, an extra chair
to prepare
a welcome for all
our dearly departed,

might have woken
this morning
to look for footprints

in cold ashes, a kiss
of bluish lips
on shiny rims

had I not ventured
against all wisdom
handed down
last night to wander
through the thinning veil
under hunchbacked husks
lurking in the banksia's withered clutches
amongst the darkening
lanes of our neighbourhood
beyond the brush
and drift,
the glimmering suspension
of nightfall, to seek the hiss
and whisper
of a hundred bluish lips
and gather up whatever
wayward spirits might decide
to follow—

too long waiting for my own
to find me here,
so far, too far
from home.

(*Samhain* is the ancient Celtic feast of the dead, still observed
by many people of Gaelic origin.)

Ghost fishing

by Heather Bourbeau

Last week on the Bonneville Salt Flats—
human hair, gum, messages of love, a fly dead,
feet stuck between the crystals.

Back home, my persimmon that did not fruit
drops leaves of deep orange and rust.
My ache for taut honey flesh softened.

The lavender and white sage have taken root
among the petrichor. Fire season over,
I can almost be forgiven this moment of hope.

I make plans to fly with friends to Lapland.
On the news, the young shame those of us
who still feel such things.

I have dreams in which I cannot breathe.
No one sees I am choking.
Rescue is not an option.

("Ghost fishing" is the continued capture of organisms in
lost, abandoned, or discarded fishing gear.)

Tawny frogmouths

by Anne Casey

Bucking plummeting numbers,
clustered at dusk—
braced against a stiff westerly
on a teeming branch
of the jacaranda—
two tiny tight-lipped
shut-eyed fluff-bundles
huddle up to their mother,
with her one yellow eye
primed, silver-grey plumage
simmering against
the snakeskin bark, a solitary
male back-to-back
with his brood
bringing up the rear

as we cluster with our sons,
goggle-eyed beneath
purple bells flying,
in stunned gratitude—
reluctant to budge
lest we break the spell.

As I struggle to be grateful for even the oxalis overtaking my garden once again

by Heather Bourbeau

I.

Today, we will gather outside,
say brief thanks, share bounty
baked and brined. Jackets and gloves.
Selfishly, we will thank gods for the dry.

Tomorrow, we will pray for rain.
We will have leftovers, complain
of bellies too full. Groomed to
Augustus Gloop, drown in chocolate.

II.

Today, hand in butter, I stare out at my garden,
make mental list to rip from roots
oxalis, nasturtiums, wayward vines
before I see the rose. Yellow. Audacious.

Fragrant. Out of season. A summons.
To honor the testament to water,
hail the return of spiders and worms
to a lush, low lying green.

A young camper will brag,
"I have already kissed five banana slugs,
and I am only seven."
I will see how blind I have been,
how much I need to catch up.

Chasing ghosts

by Anne Casey

Crossing over the broad
silver shimmer of the Hawkesbury River,
its ethereal glow under a low-lying
solid granite sky,
a door flies open
as the swarm and throng
of Sydney's silhouette fills my rear-view
for the first time in ten months,
the half-life of a pandemic (so far at least).

Cruising up the coast
to chase ghosts of girls
I've pursued for four years,
I take in the sweet, piney outbreath
of Eucalypts brimming every which way,
pressing thick bundles of ruddy
new hope to mask
the dark scars of
the last megafires, their black
tideline still visible at intervals
between drifts of blanching mist
where seventy-metre high flame fronts
had leapt this freeway.

I have come to find Margaret—
a century and a half too late
to save her, dead at fifteen from indifference—
interred somewhere in the grounds
of Christ Church,

its spiked spine
and piercing spires now stabbing
at the ashen, overstuffed
underbelly of the sky,

the air muggy
with a jumbled perfume
of brine, star jasmine,
frangipani and magnolia as
I navigate the tidy path
past a spruce
war memorial to the soaring
voices of an adolescent choir
floating from an open window,
between weather-worn
tombstones mossy
with wraiths—

I press aside
a swell of coastal rosemary
to find Hannah at thirty-eight:
Weep not husband, children dear,
John, struck down at the same age:
while at work in a pit bore-hole,

under the grey beards and many
hooded eyes of a gnarled banksia:
Annie, *beloved daughter*
aged five years and eight months,
alongside Jessie, *two years and five months,*
forever loved

beneath a stand
of sprawling figs,

last living witnesses
to Margaret's committal—
Young as this child is,
she was in a frightful state
of disease prevalent amongst
her sex and class of older years—
their broad glossy leaves
alert now in the unearthly
stillness, knuckled limbs
heavy with bequests
of sea-green teardrops,
some bursting, crimson-hearted,
sticky in the dead heat,

a stumble over knobbly
roots branching
between plots,
their leathered phalanges
caressing the edges
of stone too weathered to read
before plunging under
the pulp-strewn earth,
their testaments withheld—

a high melancholic cry
among the branches
as I stop to take in
this glorious light breaking through
along the golden tideline below,
black crows of surfers
bobbing in the midline,
and above a rolling navy hull,
a swollen white mainsail

running full-clip across
the spectral surface of the bay,
the brooding bulks
of coal-ships haunting
the misty horizon
as I find
no trace of my Margaret here,

a flurry of lorikeets
splitting the air
with their impish
See here! See here!
a tinge of coastal rosemary
lingering for a while
on my fingers
as the veil descends again
this last day of November
on the long drive home.

Relocations

by Heather Bourbeau

Lulled in flannel and wool, I deny
what my nose first finds—the spray of skunk
peeling my dreams. Dichotomous demands:
attention and revulsion.

In another four hours,
when the sun finally rises to burn
sulfuric acid suspended in fog,
I will search, booted and bitter, for burrows.

The yuletide irony is not lost—
Songs of comfort and joy and mangers permeate,
while I comb my garden for a polyamorous nook
I have every intention of destroying.

You have to drive a skunk far, farther
than you thought—farther than I drove my ex
to catch a plane, our fate known only to me, in my bones,
as we shared those last moments so close and so apart.

Otherwise, the skunk can find its way back. Fixated.
Before a skunk releases its scent, it will
stamp, snarl, spit, click its teeth, raise its tail.
So many warnings, for those who can read the signs.

Season's greetings

by Anne Casey

We have left
the wettest November on record,
crossed the invisible threshold of December.

Small blunt-edged stars
string plastic jollity from
the frangipani—still
refusing to bloom.
The flamingo lily
has sprung a single
shrivelled bloodshot aureole,
the first Christmas beetle
belly-up in a puddle
at its feet.

In a rare outburst yesterday, the dog
launched feet-first yelping at the fence.
A crash high in the palm as I ventured
to investigate, loyal hound quivering at my shin,
as a massive snake clattered through fronds
to the ground, arrow head held high,
olive back zigzagging over sandstone—
a flash of yellow underbelly
as it vanished through
a gap in the fence.

An hour after, the dog
had returned outside:
nose twitching skyward,
dropping to the landing site

then mapping the winding trail
to the snake's exit point. Over and over,
his small head followed the same course
while he stood planted under the palm.
Next day, he was there replaying it again.

I might talk of portents,
how we are stuck on repeat
as omicron cases double every two days,
our Health Minister warning of blistering records
to come—our 'other' home, family again on the wrong side
of a closed border, but for now, I have turned my gaze
to a rare break—blue sky spilling sunlight, branches thick
with shining green stars, wattles decked in golden garlands,
where the first cicadas of summer are chirping
their song of freedom from the bogged earth.

Solstice

by Heather Bourbeau

Here we are tilted as far from the sun as can be.
Even the waning moon has pulled away.
This Cold Moon, Bitter Moon, Oak Moon apogee.
My days will grow longer now.

What will we remember from this time?
This relentless distance.
Breath caught in mask.
Denials. Acceptances.

I swab my nose.
Five slow circles left, right. Wait.
This is my meditation now.
This attendance to my vigilance and vulnerability.

I stream wetland sounds
as I wait for birds to wake.
I hold my hand against my heart and say,
"I see your suffering. I am sorry."

Christmas Day 2021

by Anne Casey

> "a great day for planet Earth"
> — Bill Nelson, NASA Administrator

Bright cone piercing the grey heavens,
twin white fire-wings thrusting out of dense, green rainforest,
the James Webb Space Telescope launches from French Guiana
on its million-mile journey to halo-orbit the sun,
bear witness to the birth of our universe,
probe the dawn of starlight.

I sit on our bed
gazing out across the evening garden
as I tap my father's number.
His voice is sleep-thick, warming instantly
against the screeching sea wind
as he pulls the blanket over
the morning chill.
Over our fence, a flock
of peace lilies stand to attention:
erect on their stork-legs,
swan-bodies poised,
heron-bills lancing
the cooling air
as he makes light
of my hopes to journey
home *in a month or so—*
when things settle down,
a sick ache swelling like
the rain-bloated wattles brushing

dusk-light along our northern skyline.
He will spend the day alone
(not for want of invitations),
stubborn in his own exile.
A last wash of soft peach
filters between dimming branches
as we gloss over the blurriness of daily news,
return to his sure ground of times past.

The James Webb will spend five years
tracking light to look 13.5 billion years back.
I have spent two years deflecting darkness
to look forward, wedged between generations,
behind locked borders—shielding with my children
half the earth from my father, too afraid
now to reflect five years
into the future.

Hours later,
awake in the sleeping house,
I press aside the blinds—
somewhere far overhead
in the darkness, the James Webb
has shed its fairing to emerge for the first time
into space and, though I can't see them, I know
they are there, upraised in the dense gloom—
the neighbours' luminous peace lilies,
ivory cones probing the dank air,
white wings uplifted, waiting faithfully
for the return of light.

Awards and recognition for poems by Heather Bourbeau in this book

—'Pause' was awarded Honorable Mention in Poetry for the *2021 Soul-Making Keats Literary Competition.*

Acknowledgements for poems by Heather Bourbeau in this book

Versions of these poems appeared in the following:

—'This is not an inauguration poem' was first published in *The Coop*, January 2022.

—'Richter's scale' and 'Stow away' were first published in *Migozine*, Summer 2021.

—'Pause' was first published in *The Hopper*, Fall 2021.

—'Perigee' was first published in *MAYDAY*, November 2021.

—'Kin' was first published in *Thimble Literary Magazine*, Vol. 4, No. 3, 2021.

—'Congregation' was first published in *Trasna*, September 2022.

Awards and recognition for poems by Anne Casey in this book

—'Our Prime Minister says the vaccine is not a silver bullet' was awarded 1st Prize in the *American Writers Review Competition 2021.*

—'It is the first of winter' was awarded 2nd Prize in the *New York Encounter Poetry Contest 2022.*

—'Some days you're the seed, some days the bird' was Highly Commended in the *Galway University Hospitals Arts Trust 'Poems for Patience' Competition 2022.*

—'Christmas Day 2021' was Commended in the *WB Yeats Poetry Prize 2022* (WB Yeats Society of Victoria, Australia).

—'By afternoon's slanting' was shortlisted for the *Bridport Prize 2021*.

—'Conversations with my father' was shortlisted for the *Anthology Poetry Award 2021*.

—'Season of Samhain' was a Semi-Finalist in the the *Pablo Neruda Prize for Poetry 2022 (Nimrod Journal)*.

—'Christmas Day 2021' was shortlisted for *The Plough Prize 2022* and longlisted for the *Fish Poetry Prize 2022*.

—'The stillness of dying' and 'Autumn shades' were longlisted for the *Bridport Prize 2021*.

—'Some days you're the seed, some days the bird' was longlisted for *The Plough Prize 2021*.

—'The Minister for Bushfire Recovery is reassigned to Floods' was longlisted for the *Live Canon International Poetry Prize 2021*.

Acknowledgments for poems by Anne Casey in this book

—'Coastal descant' was first published in *American Writers Review 2021*.

—'Our Prime Minister says the vaccine is not a silver bullet' was first published in *American Writers Review 2021*.

—'Some days you're the seed, some days the bird' was first published in *American Writers Review 2021*. It was subsequently published in *Australian Poetry Anthology*, Vol 9, 2021-2022.

—'The federal government has extended the international border ban until June' was first published in *Southerly Journal*, Vol. 79.3, 2022.

—'The Minister for Bushfire Recovery is reassigned to Floods' was first published in the *Live Canon Prize Anthology 2021*.

—'Evensong' was first published in *Trasna*, September 2022.

—'It is the first of winter' was first published as part of the *New York Encounter 2022* cultural conference at Metropolitan Pavilion in New York City in February 2022.

—'To see an owl in the day, wisdom must come' was first published in *Antipodes Journal*, Vol. 34.2, 2022.

—'Tawny frogmouths' was first published in the *The Canberra Times* in August 2022.

—'Season of Samhain' was first published in *Nimrod Journal*, Fall 2022.

—'Storming our perimeters' was published in the *Stony Thursday Book 2022*.

—'Our Prime Minister says the vaccine is not a silver bullet' and 'It is the first of winter' were published in the September 2022 issue of *The Journal*, the official publication of the Australian Irish Heritage Association.

Heather Bourbeau is an American writer whose creative work has appeared in 100 Word Story, *Alaska Quarterly Review*, *The Kenyon Review*, *Meridian*, *The Stockholm Review of Literature*, and SWWIM. Her work has been featured in several anthologies, including *America, We Call Your Name: Poems of Resistance and Resilience* (Sixteen Rivers Press) and *RESPECT: The Poetry of Detroit Music* (Michigan State University Press). She has worked with various UN agencies, including the UN peacekeeping mission in Liberia and UNICEF Somalia. Her forthcoming collection "Monarch" (Cornerstone Press, 2023) is a poetic memoir of overlooked histories from the American West she was raised in.

heatherbourbeau.com

@hfbourbeau

Anne Casey is an Irish poet/writer living in Australia and author of four previous poetry collections. A journalist, magazine editor, legal author and media communications director for 30 years, her work ranks in leading national daily newspaper, *The Irish Times'* Most Read, and is widely published and anthologised internationally. Anne has won literary prizes in Ireland, the UK, the USA, Canada, Hong Kong and Australia, most recently *American Writers Review 2021* and the 2021 *iWoman Global Award for Literature*. She is the recipient of an Australian Government Scholarship for her PhD in Creative Writing at the University of Technology Sydney.

anne-casey.com

@1annecasey

Praise for this book

"Lyrical ballads for our fraught and troubled decade, Heather Bourbeau and Anne Casey's *Some Days The Bird* recasts the great Wordsworth and Coleridge double-act into the language of our day. Conversing across continental time-shifts between North America and Australia, from garden to garden, window to window, the abundant contrary states of seasons and politics are released amid the drumbeat of the pandemic. *Some Days The Bird* is a powerful record of all our recent lives.

Dealing with the daily pressures of isolation, the minutiae of nature becomes an unsentimental refuge as the separate pasts of both poets' experiences of family and country are inscribed in these clear-eyed, accessible and 'spoken' poems. The ecology of our world is matched by the ecology of physical life focussing upon women's lives and bodies, turning this conversation between two poets into a powerfully rendered portrait of our age. This is an important book. Never sombre or introverted, but full of the magic of naming things – birdlife, trees, the landscapes of home and the territories of memory – *Some Days The Bird* is essential, radiant reading."

**Gerald Dawe, Poet and Fellow Emeritus,
Trinity College Dublin**

"A complex and layered collection, *Some Days The Bird* by Heather Bourbeau and Anne Casey embraces the wonders of nature while both poets react to and survive a world-wide pandemic. The world has shrunk under the confines of lockdown, yet these exquisite meditations shared between writerly friends and based in meticulous observation express the expansive and redeeming power that poetry can provide even when humans must physically distance themselves from others. From cataloguing lush gardens teeming with life ('Some days you're the seed, some days the bird' and 'Watching the grass grow') to witnessing nature's deadly force due to climate change ('The Minister for Bushfire Recovery is reassigned to Floods' and 'Days of wild weather') the collection demonstrates how human connection remains possible through our connection to the natural landscape. Every flower, every creature, every raindrop Bourbeau and Casey observe entwines writer and reader together, without need for masking or distancing. *Some Days The Bird* is luscious poetry at its best, rich and satisfying, and at all points luminous."

JC Reilly, Managing Editor, *Atlanta Review*

"This work is both deeply serious and also powerfully playful in the very best way. Casey and Bourbeau, in a deeply engaged poetic conversation, are not afraid to be clear-eyed about what is occurring in our COVID-world but their attention to precise details, to an almost reverent naming of seemingly ordinary garden processes, makes these beautifully observed moments quite extraordinary. These are poems which use language in ever inventive ways: 'Tawny frogmouths' are 'two tiny tight-lipped shut-eyed fluff-bundles'; an 'overhanging fog' is one that swathes with a 'seductive' trousseau. We see serendipitous 'Nasturtiums never planted sprout and spill' and we witness clusters of 'wind-seeded crocus' as these two poets turn their eye to the necessary and uplifting idea that we are not quite done yet, even while their lament is what makes their work all the more resonant. Essential reading."

Siobhan Campbell, Poet, Critic and Academic, Senior Lecturer of Creative Writing, The Open University

"In *Some Days The Bird*, all that is Anthropocene, broken, and damned becomes sensuously palpable, painfully suffocating, and hot to the touch. Bourbeau and Casey seek not to cure or make whole with pacifying cliché, but rather to engage each other (and fortunately the reader) in the slivers of beauty that occasionally wind through bitter despair, death, injustice, and sorrow. We are flies on their wall, swatter-smashed by the truth in verse that is the poet's great charge. Here in fragments of feathers across oceans and continents, it lives inspirationally in *Some Days.*"

J. Drew Lanham, Poet and Distinguished Professor of Wildlife Ecology, Clemson University

"This florescent poetry conversation lifts the reader out of the wastes into the possibility of a renewal and fecundity that are not trapped in systems of oppression or prescriptive readings of nature, body or planet. Heather Bourbeau and Anne Casey speak across the world, garden to garden, local experience to local experience, and across the traumas of pandemic and the disasters of the climate crisis, with a sensitive awareness of the impacts the dramatic ecological changes are having on the planet. This is an enduring private and public lyrical interaction, that neither obscures the brutal truths nor fails to observe and record the brilliance of life in its myriad forms."

John Kinsella, Poet, Novelist, Critic, Essayist, Emeritus Professor of Literature and Environment, Curtin University

Some Days The Bird

Printing was completed in November 2022 for Beltway Editions.

Beltway
EDITIONS